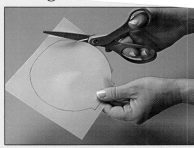

1. Cut shape from translucent Vellum to create illusion of looking through glass or liquid.

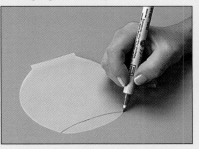

2. To make edges more visible, use brush tip water based marker to draw a fine line along edges of Vellum shape.

3. To soften marker lines, use a foam applicator or cotton swab to shade edges of Vellum with chalk.

4. Prepare background of album page or card. Arrange and glue shapes in desired design. Working on wrong side of Vellum shape, place tiny dots of 2-Way glue along edges so marker lines hide them. Glue Vellum shape on page.

Happiness is Having a Pet - Pale Blue and Sparkle vellum • Red dot with 3 leaves and Gray dot paper • Cardstock (Black, White, Deep Red, Gold, Charcoal Gray) • Album page • Black ⅝" letter stickers • Deckle and Jumbo Scallop scissors • Punches (½" and ¾" hearts for ears, ⅛" circle for eyes, ¼" circle for foot pads, 5/16" circle for nose and foot pads, ¾" circle for muzzle, 1" circle for paws, 2" circle for fish, ⅜" heart for fish) • Templates or patterns (3¾" oval for body, 2" heart cut in half for legs, 2" circle for head and tail) • Blue brush tip marker • Blue chalk

Tail Pattern

Large Fish Bowl Pattern for Scrapbook Page

Note: Reduce Bowl Pattern to 75% for Card

Forever Friends Card - Pale Blue and Sparkle vellum • 8½" x 11" sheet of White vellum for envelope (pattern on page 14) • Red dot with 3 leaves and Gray dot paper • Cardstock (White, Deep Red, Black, Yellow, Charcoal Gray) • Black ½" letter stickers • Scissors (Deckle, Scallop, Stamp) • Punches (7/16" and 3/16" hearts for ears, ⅛" and ¼" circles for foot pads and nose, ⅝" circle for muzzle, ¾" circle for paws, ⅜" heart for fish, 1¼" circle for fish) • Templates or patterns (2½" oval for body, 1½" circle for head and tail, 1¾" heart cut in half for legs) • Black and Light Blue brush tip water based markers • Blue chalk

Magic with Vellum Translucents 3

Vellum Overlays

Achieve the look of glass or water easily and quickly with translucent vellum. The layers add realistic depth and dimension to the designs. Add slices of lemon for garnish and like magic, 'The Good Old Summer Time' has arrived!

Summertime Page - K & C Company Floral Pearl embossed vellum • Yellow and Pale Blue vellum • Turquoise fleck and Turquoise dot paper • Cardstock (White, Pale Yellow, Bright Yellow, Orange) • Album page • Corkscrew and Deckle scissors • 1¼" circle punch cut into eights • 1⅜" and 1⅝" circle templates or patterns for rind • White gel pen • Black marker • Blue chalk Cut eight ¾" squares from Blue vellum for ice cubes. Cut White ¼" x 5⅛" rectangle for straw. Line rim of pitcher and glass with gel pen.

TIPS: Cut slit in lemon slice and place on top of glass. Slit glass and insert straw.

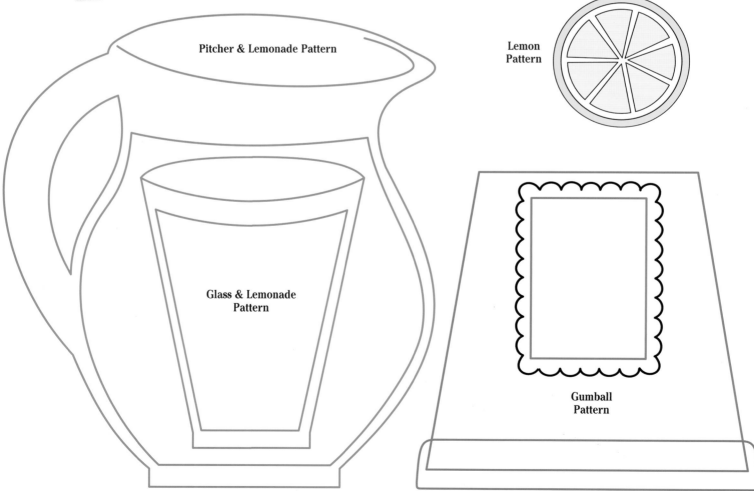

Heart Folding for Butterflies & Flowers

1. Punch a Yellow 2" heart.

2. Fold heart over at center.

3. Open flat with center fold raised to front.

4. Fold toward the center.

5. Repeat for other side.

6. Finished heart.

Butterflies Overlay - Vellum (Medium Blue, Red, Yellow, Dark Green) • Design Originals butterflies paper • Cardstock (Black, Yellow, White) • Green grass die cut • Album page • ⅝" Light Blue letter stickers • Cloud scissors • Punches (¾" heart, 1¼" heart, 2" heart, ⁵⁄₁₆" circle, ½" star, ⅝" spiral) • Pink brush tip water based marker • Fuchsia chalk
TIPS: Punch three 1¼" and three 2" Yellow hearts for each butterfly. Cut one heart of each size in half. Outline edges with pen and shade with chalk. Fold all hearts in half, open and fold edges of uncut hearts to meet at center crease. Body is 1¼" Black heart cut in half. Punch and cut in half 2" Green heart for leaves. Large flower is made from five 1¼" Red hearts. Medium flower is made from three ¾" hearts. Small flower is made from two ¾" Red hearts. Fold and crease hearts. Cut a ³⁄₁₆" x 4" rectangle from Dark Green for center flower stem.

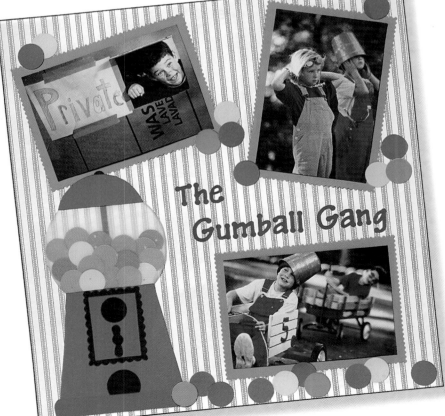

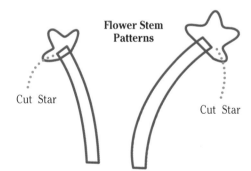

Flower Stem Patterns

Cut Star   Cut Star

Gumball Gang Page - Sparkle vellum • Red ticking stripe paper • Cardstock (Green, Blue, Yellow, Red, Orange, Charcoal Gray) • Album page • Red ¾" letter stickers • Scallop and Stamp scissors • Punches (⅝" heart cut in half for handle, ⁵⁄₁₆" circle for handle, ¾" circle for gumballs and change slot, 1" circle for gumball slot) • Circle templates (3½" for glass ball, 2½" cut in half for top) • Blue brush tip water based marker • Blue chalk
Use a ⁵⁄₁₆" circle for top of gumball machine and a ³⁄₁₆" x 2½" strip of Charcoal Gray for center shaft inside glass ball.

Gumball Pattern

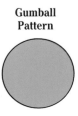
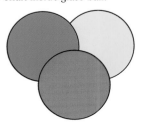

1. To make ruffle: Cut ¾" wide strips of vellum. Glue strips together end to end. Use decorative scissors to trim one long edge of strip.

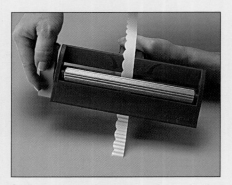

2. Run the vellum strip through the paper crimper.

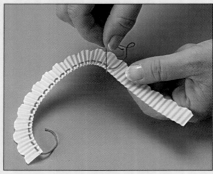

3. Using needle and embroidery floss, sew a running stitch through every other pleat. Shape lace to fit photo or greeting card by pressing crimped edges close together on inside edge of lace. Adjust thread so lace lies flat.

Sturdy Vellum becomes dainty lace when you scallop the edges and run it through a paper crimper… a perfect technique for all your romantic projects.

Envelope Pattern on page 14.

Get Well Card - Art Impressions Red heart buds vellum • White vellum • Pink ticking stripe paper • Cardstock (White, Rose Fleck, Rose Pink, Pale Pink, Forest Green, Yellow) • Dark Green ⅝" letter stickers • Scissors (Cloud, Stamp, Scallop) • Punches (⅝" maple leaf, ⅜" heart, ¼" sun and ¹⁄₁₆" circle) • Paper crimper • Red Metallic embroidery floss
Envelope - Red Heart Buds vellum • Cardstock (White, Rose Fleck, Rose Pink, Pale Pink, Forest Green, Yellow) • Punches (⅝" maple leaf, ⅜" heart and ¼" sun)

Create fabulous pages and invitations with this clever ruffle made of Vellum.

Wedding Page - Art Impressions Red heart buds vellum • White vellum • Pink ticking stripe paper • Cardstock (Rose Fleck, Deep Pink, Pale Pink, Forest Green, Yellow, Gold) • Album page • Dark Green ⅝" letter stickers • Scissors (Cloud, Stamp, Jumbo Scallop) • Punches (1½" maple leaf, ½" heart, ⅝" sun, ¼" sun, ¾" circle, ⅛" circle) • Paper crimper • Red Metallic embroidery floss TIPS: For flower, glue 5 punched hearts to ¾" circle of same color. Glue ⅝" and ¼" punched suns to center.

Lace Effects

Inside or out, there's no place like home. Here lace borders and white eyelet curtains spruce up these lovely dimensional scrapbook pages.

Fold

Window Page
Curtain Pattern

8½"

Cut here for first curtain.

Cut here for second curtain.

Flower Garden Page - 2 sheets of Hot off the Press field of flowers vellum • Vellum (Medium Green, White, Striped White) • Bright Yellow cardstock • Album page • White ¾" letter stickers • 1/16" and 1/8" circle punches • Mini Pop Dots • Scallop scissors
TIP: Cut butterflies and a few flowers from second sheet of flower vellum. Use pop dots to attach cutouts over same design on first sheet.

Heart Pattern

Open the window to reveal the photo of Mom, Dad and Baby.

Window Page - Vellum (White striped for curtain, White Marbled for window, White for lace) • 2 sheets of Design Originals Home Style Bricks paper • Moss Green and Ivory cardstock • Fleck cardstock (Burgundy, Forest Green, Rose, Rust) • Album page • Dark Green 3/4" letter stickers • Scallop scissors • Punches (1/16" circle, 1/8" circle, 1 1/4" heart, 1 1/4" tulip)

TIPS: Glue 6 1/4" x 8 1/2" Ivory photo mat to brick paper. Center and glue 5 1/2" x 7 3/4" Burgundy mat to Ivory mat. Glue 1/4" wide dividers to 6 3/4" x 8 1/2" window frame and window glass and curtains to back of window. Glue hinged portion of window frame on left of mats. Glue 2" x 8 1/2" shutter on each side of window. Punch hearts from brick paper, glue on shutters. Glue 1/2" x 7 1/4" window sill under window.

Tulip Pattern

Note: Cut 2 Tulip Patterns Reverse 1.

Leaf Pattern

Flower Pot Pattern

Window Frame Diagram Front View

6 3/4"

Score & Fold

8 1/2"

Total left side width, 1 1/4". From left edge to fold 1/2".

Note: Cut a vertical window strip 1/4" x 7 1/2". Cut a horizontal window strip 1/4" x 5 1/2". Glue strips to back of window.

Top, right side and bottom 3/4" width.

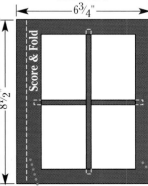

1. Use a pencil to lightly draw guidelines or use template to draw shape on wrong side of vellum. Cut along pencil line with decorative scissors. Erase pencil lines.

2. Different looks can be achieved by turning scissors over. Cut sand with cloud scissors right side up. Cut waves with cloud scissors turned over.

3. For even continuous design, align blade design with previous cut. Do not cut to very end of scissors. For an uneven design, shift or misalign blade pattern making some scallops longer and fuller than others.

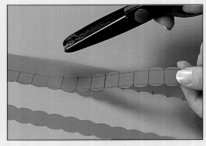

4. Cut a border strip by making second cut parallel to first cut forming a mirror image. Draw pencil guidelines to help line up cuts.

Decorative scissors are one of the scrapbooker's most useful tools. Use them to make borders, mats and decorative elements for your pages. Turn them over... and cut a whole new design.

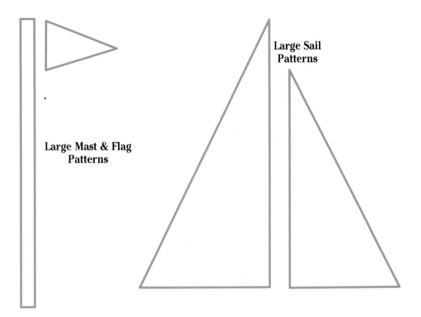

Large Mast & Flag Patterns

Large Sail Patterns

Sand and sea have never been more fun... you can almost hear the gulls calling!

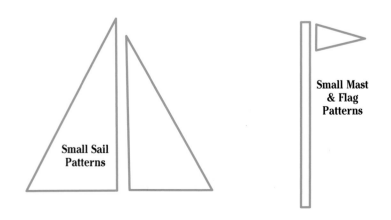

Small Sail Patterns

Small Mast & Flag Patterns

Large Sun Face Pattern

Small Sun Face Pattern

Envelope Pattern on page 14.

Translucent Vellum is the perfect look for stunning clouds and sails.

Sea, Sand & Surf - Vellum (Beige, Tan, Dark Blue, Medium Blue, White, Yellow, Gold, White Marbled) • Light Blue ticking stripe and Red stripe paper • Cardstock (Red, Tan, White) • Album page • White ⅝" letter stickers • Scissors (Jumbo Scallop for seagulls, Zig-zag for sun, Deckle and Jumbo Deckle for mats, Cloud for sand, waves and clouds) • 1¼" circle punch for sun • 2¾" and 3" oval templates for clouds • Circle templates or patterns (2" and 1¼" for sun, 3¼" cut portion for boat) • Red and Black markers
TIP: Cut sand, waves and clouds with cloud scissors using uneven pattern.

Bon Voyage - Vellum (White Marbled, Medium Blue, White, Gold, Yellow, Dark Blue, Tan, Beige) • Light Blue ticking stripe and Red stripe paper • Cardstock (White, Red, Tan) • 4½" x 6¼" folded White cardstock card • White ½" letter stickers • Scissors (Jumbo Deckle, Scallop, Zig-zag, Cloud) • Circle punches (2" for boat, 1" for sun) • 1½" and 1¼" circle templates for sun • 1⅝" and 1⅞" oval templates for clouds • Red and Black markers
TIP: Start with 6" x 9" White cardstock card. Glue 4½" x 6 rectangle of Blue stripe paper on front of card. Use deckle scissors to cut 6¼" x 9¼" rectangle of Blue vellum. Fold in half and wrap around card base.
Envelope - 8½" x 11" sheet of Medium Blue vellum

Just look what can be done with wonderful decorative craft scissors. They come in Stamp, Scallop, Cloud, Corkscrew, and Deckle edges to name a few. Not only that, different looks can be achieved just by turning the scissors over!

Santa Face Pattern

Fold

Baby Page - White Pearl and Royal Blue vellum • Baby Blue and Medium Blue cardstock • Album page • Scissors (Stamp, Jumbo Scallop, Clouds, Seagull) • Punches (heart border, filmstrip border, ⅛" circle, 1" flower) • White gel pen
TIPS: Cut White and Royal Blue vellum strips with decorative scissors. Punch designs in some strips. Glue vellum strips on Baby Blue background. To reduce time spent gluing strips, run strips through a Zyron machine.

Vellum makes a unique see-thru background for very special pages.

Our Family - Translucent vellum • Blue dot background and scraps of Red print paper for hearts • Red cardstock • Album page • Red and White heart block letter stickers • Corkscrew scissors • 1¼" heart punch

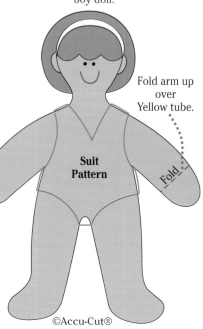

Wet & Wild Doll Pattern
Use same body for boy doll.

Fold arm up over Yellow tube.

Suit Pattern

Fold

©Accu-Cut®

Crimped Vellum

Cut out hole on Whisker Pattern here for face pattern to go behind.

Whisker Pattern

Mustache Pattern
Glue Mustache over Whisker Pattern

Fold

Wet and Wild - Vellum (Medium Blue, Dark Blue, White) • Design Originals Deep Blue Sea and Red stripe paper • Cardstock (Light Blue, Red, Brown, Rust, Lime Green, Yellow, Brown Kraft) • Album page • Three Accu-Cut 3¼" paper dolls • Red, White and Blue patriotic block letter stickers • Scissors (Cloud, Corkscrew, Stamp, Scallop, Deckle) • Circle punches (¼" for ears, ½" for bun, ¾" for hair, 1" for hair and tube center, 2" for tube) • Paper crimper • Red and Black markers • Pink chalk

Christmas Page - Hot off the Press hearts and dots vellum • Vellum (White, Red, Dark Green) • Red dot paper • Cardstock (Black, Red, Kelly Green, White, Flesh) • Album page • Cloud and Deckle scissors • Punches (1" sun for pompon, ¼" circle for eyes and berries, ½" circle for nose, 1¼" holly) • Templates or patterns (5" heart for bottom beard and face, 4" heart for top beard, 5¼" for whiskers, 3¾" for mustache and cap) • 1½" chubby letter stencil • Paper crimper • Pink chalk
TIP: For cap trim, use deckle scissors to cut three 1¼" x 4½" strips of White vellum. Round off ends and stack. For pompon, punch four 1" suns. Stack and glue on cap. For crimping tips, see page 14.

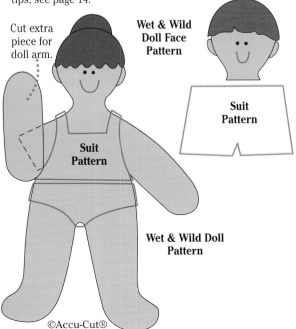

Cut extra piece for doll arm.

Wet & Wild Doll Face Pattern

Suit Pattern

Suit Pattern

Wet & Wild Doll Pattern

Crimped Vellum

Add a new wrinkle to your scrapbooks and cards. Cut vellum strips and shapes, run them through a paper crimper and you'll add texture and dimension to even the most simple design.

Fold

1. Cut shape or strip of vellum. Crimping a long strip of vellum will shorten it a little so cut strips longer than needed. Cut or punch any details that pattern requires.

2. Open jaws of crimper and place edge of vellum in crimper. Hold jaws together with one hand while turning the wheel with other hand.

Everyone just loves dressing up for Halloween. Now you can make your own matching invitations, envelopes and scrapbook pages with very little effort. Your friends and family can join in the fun!

Fold

Fold

Fold

Ghost Pattern
Reverse 1.

Use Vellum for Fun and Spooky Ghosts!

Halloween Page - Marbled vellum • Lime Green dot and Orange dot paper • Cardstock (Lime Green, Brown, Black) • Album page • Orange ¾" letter stickers • Deckle scissors • Punches (⅝" and 1¼" maple leaf, 1¼" and 2" circle for pumpkin, ⅝" spiral for stems, ⅛" circle for ghost eyes and mouth) • Paper crimper • Black marker

TIP: Punch eyes and corners of ghost mouth with ⅛" circle punch. Insert scissor tips in holes at corner of mouth to cut mouth.

Small Pumpkin & Stem Patterns

Halloween Invitation - Marbled vellum • Lime Green dot and Orange dot paper • Cardstock (Lime Green, Brown, Black) • White ½" letter stickers • Deckle scissors • Punches (1¼" and 2" circle for pumpkins, ⅝" and 1¼" maple leaf, ⅛" circle for ghost eyes and mouth, ⅝" spiral for stems) • Paper crimper • Black marker

TIP: Fold Black cardstock card. Top with Green and Black rectangles.

Envelope - 8½" x 11" sheet of spirals vellum • Lime Green dot and Orange dot paper • Brown and Lime Green cardstock • Punches (1¼" circle, ⅝" maple leaf and ⅝" spiral) • Black marker

Large Pumpkin & Stem Patterns

Torn Edges

Make natural looking trees, grass, mountains, snow and landscapes by tearing the edges of vellum. You'll be surprised by the interesting and exciting effects.

Envelope Pattern
on page 14.

To tear a straight line, place vellum on work surface. Position ruler on vellum. Press ruler down with one hand. Grasp top edge of paper between thumb and forefinger. Pull paper up and toward you. Reposition thumb and forefinger after tearing about one inch.

Star Pattern

'Tis the Season Card - White and Green vellum • Blue dot with 3 leaves and Blue dot paper • Cardstock (Burgundy Fleck, White, Tan, Black) • White ½" letter stickers • Zig-zag and Stamp scissors • Punches (¹⁄₁₆" and ¼" circle for buttons, 1¼" circle cut in half for cap, ¼" sun for pompon, ⁵⁄₈" snowflake) • Circle templates or patterns (1¼" and 2" torn for snowman) • Black and Orange markers • Blue chalk
Envelope - 8½" x 11" sheet of 48 pound vellum • Green and White vellum • ⁵⁄₈" snowflake punch • Blue chalk

Fourth of July Page - Dark Blue and Red vellum • 1½" x 6½" rectangle of Red mini star paper • Cardstock (Blue, White, Yellow) • Album page • Red, White and Blue Patriotic block letter stickers • Corkscrew scissors • Punches (⁷⁄₈" sun, ¼" star, 1" star, 1¼" star)
TIP: Tear strips of Blue vellum and glue to a full sheet of Red vellum.

Large Tree Pattern

Small Tree Pattern

Cap Pattern

Trim Pattern

Head/Face Pattern

Body/Button Pattern

Snowflake Pattern

Arms Patterns

Scarf Patterns

Medium Tree Pattern

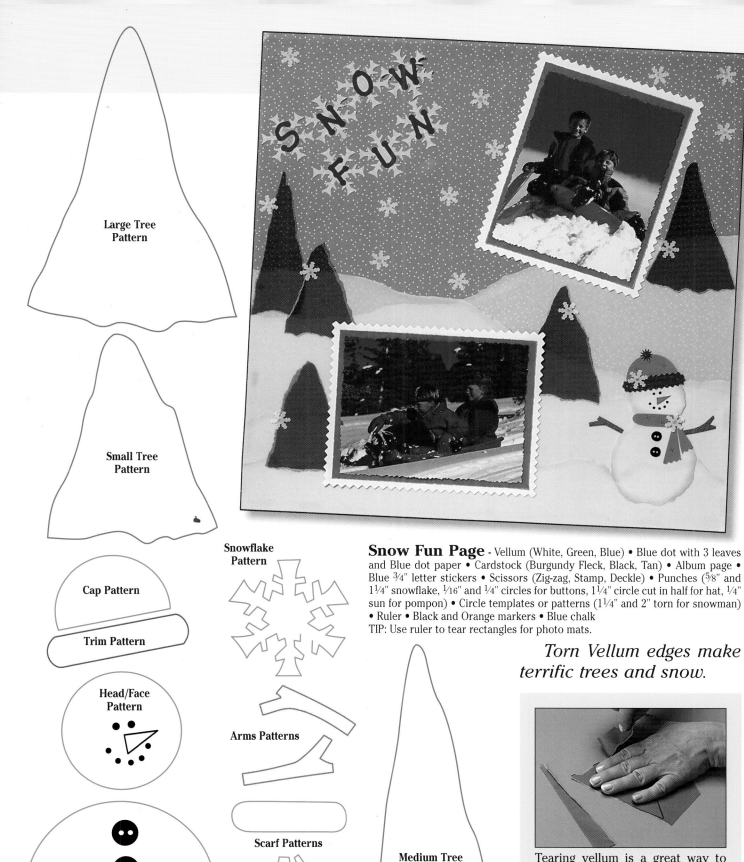

Snow Fun Page - Vellum (White, Green, Blue) • Blue dot with 3 leaves and Blue dot paper • Cardstock (Burgundy Fleck, Black, Tan) • Album page • Blue ¾" letter stickers • Scissors (Zig-zag, Stamp, Deckle) • Punches (⅝" and 1¼" snowflake, 1/16" and ¼" circles for buttons, 1¼" circle cut in half for hat, ¼" sun for pompon) • Circle templates or patterns (1¼" and 2" torn for snowman) • Ruler • Black and Orange markers • Blue chalk
TIP: Use ruler to tear rectangles for photo mats.

Torn Vellum edges make terrific trees and snow.

Tearing vellum is a great way to create scenery. Use a pencil to lightly draw guidelines. Use one hand to press vellum against work surface. With other hand grasp vellum and pull up toward you. Erase the pencil lines. Layering torn vellum is very effective.

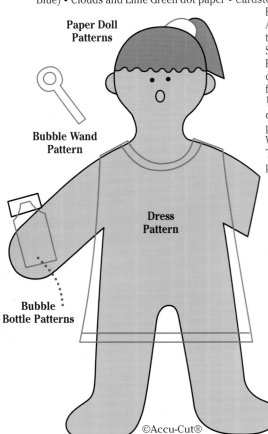

Layers of Vellum add shading to these projects.

Carrot Leaf Patterns

Carrot Patterns

Bubble Fun Page - Vellum (Dark Green, Medium Green, Pale Green, Pale Blue) • Clouds and Lime Green dot paper • Cardstock (Magenta, Yellow, Gold, Brown, Black, White) • Album page • $4\frac{1}{2}$" Accu-Cut paper doll • Blue $\frac{3}{4}$" letter stickers • Daffodil stickers • Stamp and Heartbeat scissors • Punches ($\frac{1}{2}$", $\frac{3}{4}$", 1" and $1\frac{1}{4}$" circles for bubbles, $\frac{1}{8}$" circle for flower center and bubble blower, $\frac{1}{4}$" circle for ears, $\frac{1}{4}$" flower for dress trim, $\frac{3}{4}$" heart cut in half for pony tail) • Ruler • Blue, Black and White markers • Blue chalk
TIP: Use ruler to tear rectangles for photo mats.

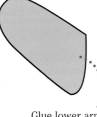

Paper Doll Patterns

Bubble Wand Pattern

Dress Pattern

Bubble Bottle Patterns

Glue lower arm on upper arm as shown in Bubble Fun Page photo.

©Accu-Cut®

Shoe Patterns Reverse 1

The Family Gardener - Vellum (Orange, Green, Moss Green, Red) • Green stripe paper • White cardstock • Album page • ¾" Dark Green letter stickers • Deckle and Jumbo Antique Elegance scissors

the family gardener

Carrot Leaf Patterns

Red Rose Leaf Patterns

Cabbage & Rose Patterns

Red Rose - Vellum (Red, Green, White) • Yellow stripe paper • Album page • ⅝" Dark Green letter stickers • Jumbo Antique Elegance and Deckle scissors

Red ROSE

Add a touch of elegance to invitations, envelopes and album pages with beautifully embossed designs.

1. A brass or vinyl stencil can be used to emboss vellum. Cut vellum to required shape and size. Place stencil right side down on work surface. Place vellum right side down on stencil. Use stylus to outline or fill in designs on stencil.

2. Vellum embossing can also be done free-hand. Cut vellum to required shape and size. Place right side down on a piece of cardboard. Use stylus to draw design. If using a pattern, place it on cardboard under vellum and trace with stylus. If you plan to use a computer to print a greeting or invitation on vellum, print it on a full sheet before cutting or embossing.

3. Working on wrong side of embossed vellum, color outlined design with brush tip water based markers. When vellum is turned right side up, the result is a soft pastel design.

Envelope Pattern on page 14.

The Smith and Denny Families

Invite you to join with them to celebrate

the Marriage of

JoAnn Smith and Andrew Denny

7:00 PM

Thursday May 10, 2001

Informal Ceremony held at the home of

John and Carol Smith

5840 Center Street

Irving, Texas

RSVP 817-282-4505

Wedding Envelope Corner Pattern

Wedding Invitation Border Pattern

The Three of Us Scrapbook Page Photo Border Pattern

Wedding Invitation - 48 pound vellum • Pink ticking stripe paper • 4⅝" x 6⅝" Moss Green Fleck cardstock • Cloud scissors • Stylus • Cardboard • Red and Green brush tip water based markers
TIP: Print invitation on computer.
Envelope - 48 pound vellum • Pink ticking stripe paper • Stylus • Cardboard • Red and Green brush tip markers
TIP: Cut out envelope and emboss before gluing together.

Lovely accents with textured Vellum.

The Three of Us
Scrapbook Page
Oval Photo
Border Pattern

The Three Of Us

The Three of Us Page - 48 pound vellum • Pink ticking stripe paper • Moss Green cardstock • Album page • Cloud scissors • Stylus • Cardboard • Red and Green brush tip water based markers
TIP: Print page title on computer. Color letters with markers. Draw thin line along edge of title and photo mats.

Photo Border
Pattern

Name Page - 48 pound vellum • Pink check paper • Rose Pink cardstock • Album page • Stylus • Stencils (border, flower mat, ¾" letter)

Name Pattern
Motif
Reverse 1.

Lisa age 2

Snowflake Pattern

Create really fabulous raised snowflakes with see-thru Vellum.

Snowflake Page - Medium Blue and 48 pound Vellum • Blue check paper • Album page • White ¾" letter stickers • Jumbo Scallop scissors • American Traditional Snowflake stencil • Stylus

Bride Pattern

Wedding Dress, Underdress & Veil Pattern

Cut here for veil.

Fold

Christening Gown & Underdress Pattern

Cut Sash

Fold

Red River

2001

Create a stunning Wedding dress or Christening gown by embossing lacy designs on translucent Vellum.

Our Day Embossing - 48 pound and White Pearl vellum • Design Originals Green Heritage floral paper • Pale Green and Honey Brown cardstock • Album page • 5¾" Accu-Cut paper doll • White ½" and ⅝" letter stickers • Flower bouquet sticker • Jumbo Scallop and Stamp scissors • Punches (¼" circle for bow center, 5/16" circle for ears, ¾" circle for bun, 1¼" circle for hair, ½" heart for bow) • Stylus • Red and Black Zig pens • Pink chalk

TIPS: Trace, emboss and cut out dress and veil using Christening dress tips. Cut ribbon trim, bow and veil from White Pearl vellum. Use the skirt of the underdress as a pattern for the veil.

Christening Page - White Pearl and 48 pound vellum • Design Originals Pink dot with 3 leaves paper • Yellow and Magenta cardstock • Album page • 5¾" paper doll • Scissors (Jumbo Scallop, Stamp, Scallop) • Punches (5/16" circle for rattle, ears and bow center, ½" circle for rattle, ½" heart for bow, ½" bow for rattle) • Stylus • Letter stencil • Red and Black markers • Pink chalk

TIPS: Position dress and bonnet pattern on cardboard. Place heavy vellum over patterns. Lightly trace outline of dress with pencil. Use stylus to emboss dress designs, scallop hem, scallop cuffs and scallops on bonnet. Cut out dress. Cut bow, ribbon dress trims and underdress from White Pearl vellum. To make hair, trace doll head on Yellow cardstock and cut with scallop scissors. Cut head and hands from doll and glue on dress. Using jumbo scallop scissors, cut a 11" strip of cardstock. Use this template to plan and emboss scalloped edges. Cut out photo and title mats.

Folded Paper Shapes

Cut and fold simple Tea-Bag squares to create stars, flowers and more!

1. Cut the vellum into the size squares you will need.

2. Fold squares diagonally matching corners and sides. Cut along one edge with decorative scissors. Open squares.

3. Fold the vellum squares as shown in diagrams.

4. Arrange or interlock folded squares. Glue together.

Fold, cut or punch Vellum shapes to make flowers, leaves and borders. These 3-dimensional embellishments bring Scrapbook pages to life.

Folding Tea-Bag Kite Shapes to Make Flower Borders

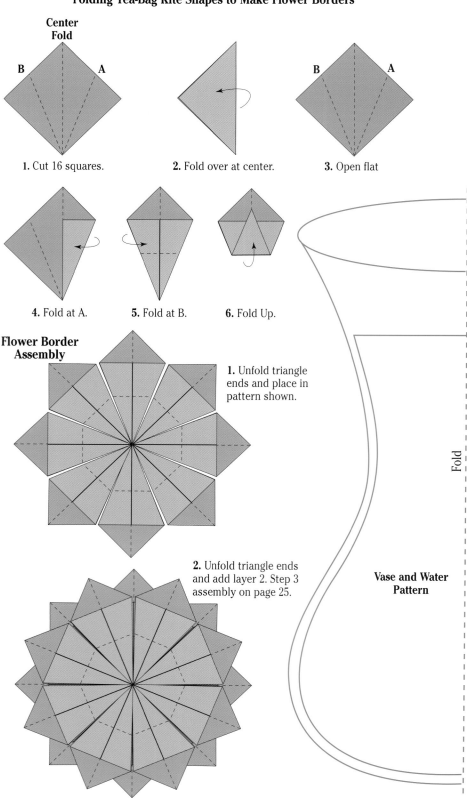

Center Fold

B   A

1. Cut 16 squares.

2. Fold over at center.

B   A

3. Open flat

4. Fold at A.

5. Fold at B.

6. Fold Up.

Flower Border Assembly

1. Unfold triangle ends and place in pattern shown.

2. Unfold triangle ends and add layer 2. Step 3 assembly on page 25.

Vase and Water Pattern

Fold

Grandma's
Little
Flowers

3. Fold up ends on alternating layers 1 and 2 to form completed flower border.

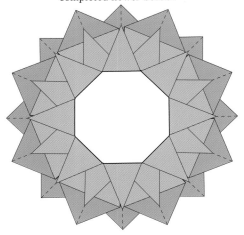

Cut a beautiful 'cut-crystal' vase from translucent printed Vellum.

Grandma's Little Flowers - Hot Off the Press swirls vellum • Vellum (Red, Yellow, Turquoise, Pale Blue, Green) • Yellow check and Fern Green paper • Album page • Red ¾" letter stickers • Scallop and Deckle scissors • White gel pen

TIPS: Each flower requires sixteen 1½" squares and the bud has three 1½" squares of vellum. Cut one 9" and two 7" flower stems for vase flowers and one 8½" stem for bud flower. Cut 3 small slots just above vase lip and insert flower stems.

Glue folded designs over top of photo on page as shown.

Fold fabulous translucent ivy leaves with green translucent Vellum.

Ivy Page - Green vellum • Lime Green stripe and White textured paper • Album page • Gold ¾" letter stickers • Deckle scissors • Green brush tip water based marker

TIP: Cut and fold 1½", nine 1¼" and six 1" Green vellum squares.

Ivy Leaf Folding Shapes

1. Cut squares.

2. Fold down.

3. Open back.

4. Fold down to middle and score.

5. Fold back again and score.

6. Repeat for other side.

7. Fold point up.

4th of July Folding Shapes

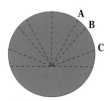

1. Cut 12 circles.

Center Fold

2. Fold up.

Center Fold

3. Turn over.

4. Fold over at center.

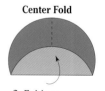

5. Open flat. Fold toward center at A.

6. Like this.

7. Fold back at B.

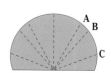

8. Fold toward center at C. Repeat for other side.

9. Finished shape.

Folded Paper Shapes

Create a glowing 'sunflower' with folded hearts made from yellow and golden translucent Vellum.

Little Sunshine Flower Folding Shapes

1. Punch a 2" heart.

2. Fold heart over at center.

3. Open flat and turn over.

4. Fold A toward the center.

5. Repeat at B for other side.

Little Sunshine - Vellum (Red, Orange, Yellow, Green) • Yellow stripe paper • Yellow cardstock • Album page • 1" and 2" heart punches • 1" Green letter stickers • Jumbo Antique Elegance scissors
TIPS: Cut twenty-four 1" Orange, twelve 2" Yellow for flowers. Cut eight 1" Green hearts, cutting in half for leaves. Cut flower stems as shown in photo. Fold edges of large hearts as shown in diagrams.

4th of July - Red and Blue vellum • Blue stripe paper • Blue cardstock • Album page • ⅝" Blue letter stickers • 2" circle punch • Jumbo Antique Elegance scissors
TIPS: Punch 12 Red and 12 Blue circles. Fold as shown.

4th of July Folding Shapes

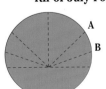

1. Cut 12 circles

2. Fold up.

Center Fold

3. Turn over.

4. Fold over at center.

5. Fold back at A.

6. Fold toward center at B.

7. Finished shape.

Markers and Chalk

Translucent Vellum butterfly shapes become miniature works of art when you draw patterns with a stylus then add color and shade them with markers and chalk.

Gather your supplies and start creating something beautiful today!

Butterflies are free to fly... soft and lovely colors adorn these happy, garden friends. Just follow these easy full size patterns to make your own creations!

1. Place pattern on a piece of cardboard. Place vellum right side down on pattern. Trace pattern with stylus.

2. Working on wrong side of embossed vellum, fill in design with brush tip markers.

3. Cut out design. Glue on album page or greeting card.

Butterfly Card - Hot Off the Press dots vellum • Vellum (Medium Green, White, 48 pound) • White 1/2" letter stickers • Cloud scissors • Film strip border punch • Stylus • Cardboard • Pastel brush tip markers
TIP: Fold dot vellum so 1" strip of Lavender cardstock shows on card front.
Envelope - 8½" x 11" sheet of Medium Green vellum

Envelope Pattern on page 14.

Color and cut beautiful butterflies from Vellum.

Mom & Me - Hot Off the Press dots vellum • Vellum (White, Light Green, 48 pound) • Lavender cardstock • Album page • White $5/8$" letter stickers • Cloud scissors • Punches (film strip border, $1/4$" heart, $1/8$" circle) • Pastel brush tip markers • Stylus • Cardboard

TIP: For lace strip, use Cloud scissors to cut $5/8$" strip of White vellum. Punch with filmstrip punch. Cut $3/16$" strip of Green vellum and weave through punched White strip.

A Walk In The Park

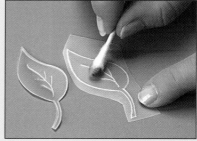

Embossed printed vellum is available. Cut out the embossed shapes. Darken colors by applying chalk to the wrong side of shapes.

A Walk in the Park -

2 sheets of K & C Company leaf embossed vellum • Beige cardstock • 5½" and two 4" Light Green cardstock square frames • Album page • Gold ⅝" letter stickers • Chalk (Pink, Green, Light Gold)

Shell Patterns

Heart Pattern

Sheep Pattern

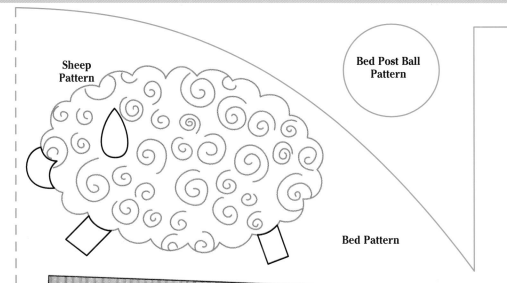

Bed Post Ball Pattern

Bed Pattern

Fold

Draw a thin line along the edge of shape using brush tip marker. Soften marker line by shading edges with chalk.

Shell Pattern

By the Sea - 48 pound vellum • Design Originals Deep Blue Sea paper • Album page • White ⅝" letter stickers • Jumbo Deckle scissors • Stylus • Cardboard • Brush tip water based markers (Lemon Yellow, Rose, Salvia Blue, Pale Green, Rosewood)

Create a beautiful page... soft sheep with embossed fur lines and delicate photo mats set the stage for peaceful sleep.

Counting Sheep - Hot Off the Press swirls vellum • Art Impressions Pink stripe vellum • Pink dot paper • Black and Wedgwood Blue cardstock • Album page • Pink ¾" letter stickers • Jumbo Scallop scissors • Punches (½" heart cut in half for ears, ¾" heart cut for face, 1¼" heart for bed, 1" circle for bedpost) • 2¾" oval template for bodies • Silver gel pen • Gray chalk

Punch Shapes

1. Punches work very well with vellum. Lubricate punches by punching through wax paper and sharpen them by punching through aluminum foil. If edges of punched shapes are rough, smooth with an emory board.

2. To accent edges of punched shapes use brush tip water based marker to draw a thin line along outside edge.

3. Soften marker line by applying a matching color of chalk to edges of punched shape.

4. For a different look, punch shapes along one edge of a sheet of vellum. Use markers and chalk around edges of punched openings. Back with bright color paper or cardstock.

Twice as Much Fun

Pink and Pale Blue vellum • Pink Gingham and Pink dots and hearts paper • Album page • Blue 3/4" letter stickers • Pink and Blue brush tip markers • Pink and Blue chalk

Fall Leaves

Full sheet of Translucent vellum • Paper (Rust plaid, Rust, Moss Green) • Album page • Leaf Block letter stickers • Jumbo Deckle scissors • Punches (1 1/4" maple leaf, 1 1/4" birch leaf, 1 1/4" oak leaf) • Dark Green brush tip water based marker • Dark Green chalk TIP: Punch leaves along one edge of vellum. Shade edges of openings. Place vellum over plaid paper. Glue a 1 1/2" wide strip of Rust cardstock under the punched leaves.

Let's Play Dress-Up - Pink vellum and 1" x 10" strip for skirt and scraps of Hot Off the Press swirls vellum for wings • Pink hearts and dots stripe and Metallic Silver paper • Cardstock (Pink, Yellow, Rose, White, Black) • Album page • Two 4½" Accu-Cut paper dolls • Pink 1" block letter stickers • Scissors (Corkscrew, Scallop, Jumbo Scallop) • Punches (¼" circle for ears, 1" circle for bangs, 1¼" circle for hair, 1¼" heart for wings, ½" star for wand, ¼" star for crown and shoes) • ¾" circle template for crown • Red and Black markers • Silver gel pen • Pink and Blue chalk

Birthday Wish Card - Pink vellum and 1" x 10" strip for skirt and scraps of Hot Off the Press swirls vellum for wings • Pink hearts and dots stripe and Metallic Silver paper • White and Yellow cardstock • 4½" Accu-Cut paper doll • Hot Pink ½" letter stickers • Scissors (Corkscrew, Scallop, Jumbo Scallop) • Punches (¼" circle for ears, 1" circle for bangs, 1¼" circle for hair, 1¼" heart for wings, ½" star for wand, ¼" star for crown and shoes) • ¾" circle template for crown • Black and Silver gel pens • Pink and Blue chalk
Envelope - Metallic Silver paper with White back • ½" and ¾" star punches
TIP: Fold envelope with White outside and Silver inside.

Wand Pattern

Face Patterns for Dress-Up Page

Doll Body for Dolls

Leotard Pattern for Dolls

Heart Wing Pattern

Envelope Pattern on page 14.

©Accu-Cut®

Punch Shapes

Bee Patterns

With a few punches and a little imagination you can make shapes to enhance all your paper designs... insects, flowers, borders, frames and more. The possibilities are endless.

Head Patterns

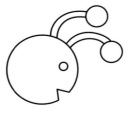

Bee Body Pattern

Bee Happy Page - Vellum (Light Blue, Medium Blue, Dark Blue, Medium Green, Dark Green) • Light Blue stripe and textured Tan paper • Cardstock (Brown, Black, Yellow) • Album page • Black ⅝" letter stickers • Corkscrew and Jumbo Deckle scissors • Punches (1¼" heart for wings, ¾" circle for head, ¼" circle for antennae, 1¼" holly for leaves, ¼" sun for flower center, ⅝" spiral for antennae and legs, 2" circle for body, 1" flower) • White gel pen • Brush tip markers (Black, Brown, Blue) • Blue chalk